IT'S FUN TO LEARN ABOUT
COLOURS

Arianne Holden
Consultant: Dr Naima Browne

ARMADILLO

NOTES

This book introduces children to colours in lively and stimulating ways. The stunning and imaginative photographs show familiar objects that will encourage a child's eagerness to learn and to participate in the hands-on activities.

Learning the basics
Children need to be able to recognize colour and learn the names first of all. They should then be able to identify the colours of things around them. Later, the ideas of shades of colour and of mixing and matching colours are introduced.

Reading together
Most children benefit from adult help when reading a book for the first time. Do not expect a child to grasp all the information in the book in one go! Go through the book at the child's pace. This will ensure that reading times are always enjoyable.

Talking it through
Talk about the things you have found out together. Make everyday activities an adventure in learning. Getting dressed, preparing meals, tidying toys and all sorts of everyday activities provide opportunities to talk about colours and to broaden your child's understanding. For example, ask questions such as – What happens to my coffee when I add milk? Can you sort the blocks into sets of colours?

Answering questions
Encourage your child to answer questions. Don't worry if the answers are wrong – making mistakes is part of the learning process. The most important thing is that your child feels confident and willing to try. Remember, of course, to praise your child when he or she answers a question correctly.

Learning by doing
Encourage your child to try all the activities. They have been specially designed to be easy and fun to do, and little preparation is required.

CONTENTS

Red

Tasty, ripe tomatoes and soft, sweet strawberries are red.

shades of red

big red hair scrunchie

What will happen to this tomato?

spicy red chillies

up ...

up and down on the red seesaw

... and down

three scuttling red crabs

Who's going to eat the juicy, red strawberries?

Did you know?

When you're shy or angry, your cheeks can turn red! Has this ever happened to you?

Green

Crisp, crunchy apples and grass are green.

shades of green

I'm hiding in the long, green grass.

Which green things am I made from?

Hop to it, hoppity green frog!

Green cactus spines are prickly. oUCH!

Try this!

Cress creature

1. Put damp cotton wool into an egg cup.

2. Scatter cress seeds and water every day.

3. Watch the cress grow.

4. Paint a face on the egg cup. Look at all that green hair!

Blue

The sea and sky are
blue on a sunny day.
Is the sky blue today?

shades of blue

two blue slithery snakes

Hisss!

A blue cap with blue bobbles.

Ted likes the colour blue.

How many
blue whales can
you count?

watch out!

three
dancing
blue aliens

There's a
blue frisbee
about!

Do you think
I can knock
down the
blue skittles?
Can you play
skittles?

Orange

Orange is a happy shade. Crunchy carrots and juicy oranges are orange.

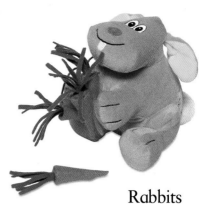
shades of orange

Rabbits love carrots.

Try this!

Make frozen orange juice

 1. Wash a small pot.

 2. Trace the top of the pot on to card.

 3. Cut it out and make a slit.

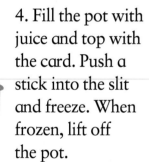 4. Fill the pot with juice and top with the card. Push a stick into the slit and freeze. When frozen, lift off the pot.

orange socks

orange trousers

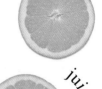
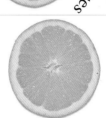

juicy oranges

orange flowers

light orange hat and bright orange t-shirt

Where did I put my orange?

Do you like eating carrots?

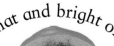

Yellow

Sour lemons and
sweet bananas
are yellow.

How many yellow
bananas has this
monkey eaten?

shades of yellow

quack ...

quack ...

quack ...

bright
yellow
ducks

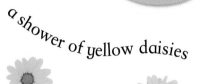

a shower of yellow daisies

disco dancing yellow corn on the cob

Try this!

Sunshine cookies

1. In a bowl, mix icing
sugar, lemon juice and
yellow food dye.

2. Spread icing on
to some cookies.

3. Can you
taste the
lemon?
Is it sweet
or sour?

Purple

Big, juicy grapes and smooth, shiny plums are purple.

shades of purple

noisy purple shakers

One ...

two ...

...three purple snails.

purple flowers tied with purple ribbon

fluttering purple butterflies

purple grapes

purple recorder

How many aubergines (eggplants) can the chef juggle?

9

Brown

Cuddly puppies, chewy toffee and muddy footprints are brown.

shades of brown

one

two

three
brown
pine
cones

Wombat's wobbly tower of brown pine cones.

a litter of brown puppies

cuddly brown Ted's cartwheeling extravaganza

muddy brown footprints

Soft, brown feathers feel ticklish.

chewy brown toffee and chocolate

Pink

Soft, sweet
marshmallows
and your
fingernails are pink.

shades of pink

What shade is your tongue?

pale pink marshmallows

bright pink bowl

rosy pink
bear

Save some
creamy, pink
pudding for me!

Try this!

Making pink dye

1. Put two
beetroots in
warm water.
Leave until the
water is pink.

2. Remove them.
Place an old white
t-shirt in the water.
Soak overnight.

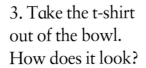

3. Take the t-shirt
out of the bowl.
How does it look?

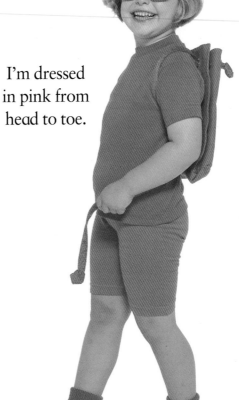

I'm dressed
in pink from
head to toe.

11

Black

You see black when you close your eyes.

What shade are these things?

A juicy black fly for a hungry black spider.

black bat mask

cool black sunglasses

Can you count ten black fingers?

Giddy-up, black ponies!

black sheriff's hat

Where are these shiny black beetles going?

black bowler hat

12

White

Snow on a cold winter's day and fluffy clouds on a summer's day are white.

Can you find any white things?

fluffy white kitten

one

two

three

frisky white lambs

Doctor Rosie will make the polar bear better.

wibbly wobbly snowman

Try this!

Make meringue snow cakes

2. Spoon cream into each meringue.

1. Whisk up some cream in a bowl.

creamy white ice cream.

Gold

Shining stars
and royal crowns
glisten like gold.

gold glitter,
thread and
crayons

glitzy
gold wig

three gold rings

two gold bangles

Look at Pirate
Ted's sparkling
gold treasure.

Try this!

Make a gold crown

1. Draw a crown shape
on to card. Cut it out.

2. Glue gold foil
on to your crown.

3. Join the ends with
adhesive tape.

I'm catching falling stars.

I've won a gold medal!

Silver

Silver is shiny.
Sometimes you can
see your reflection in
things that are silver.

silver crayons,
glitter and
thread

shiny, silver
spaceship

toot!
toot!
toot!

Astronaut Teds
wear silver
spacesuits
and helmets.

What colour are Ted's weights?

brr brr

silver
alarm
clock

Look at
my silver
fancy dress!

ticklish, silver
tinsel scarf

Bronze

Bronze is shiny. It looks a little like gold.

bronze thread and crayons

flickering bronze mirror ball

three wild, wiry bronze men

amazing magician in a bronze cloak and hat

abracadabra!

vroooom!

brilliant bronze racing cars

one

two

three

glowing bronze bows

cool bronze sunglasses

I'm a bronze robot.

dazzling bronze crown

16

Rainbow

There are seven colours in a rainbow. Do you know what they are called?

red
orange
yellow
green
blue
indigo
violet

Which rainbow colour do you like best?

ruby red

glowing orange

sunshine yellow

Ted is painting a rainbow just for you.

bows of many colours

stacking rings in rainbow colours

cool green

vivid violet

warm indigo

brilliant blue

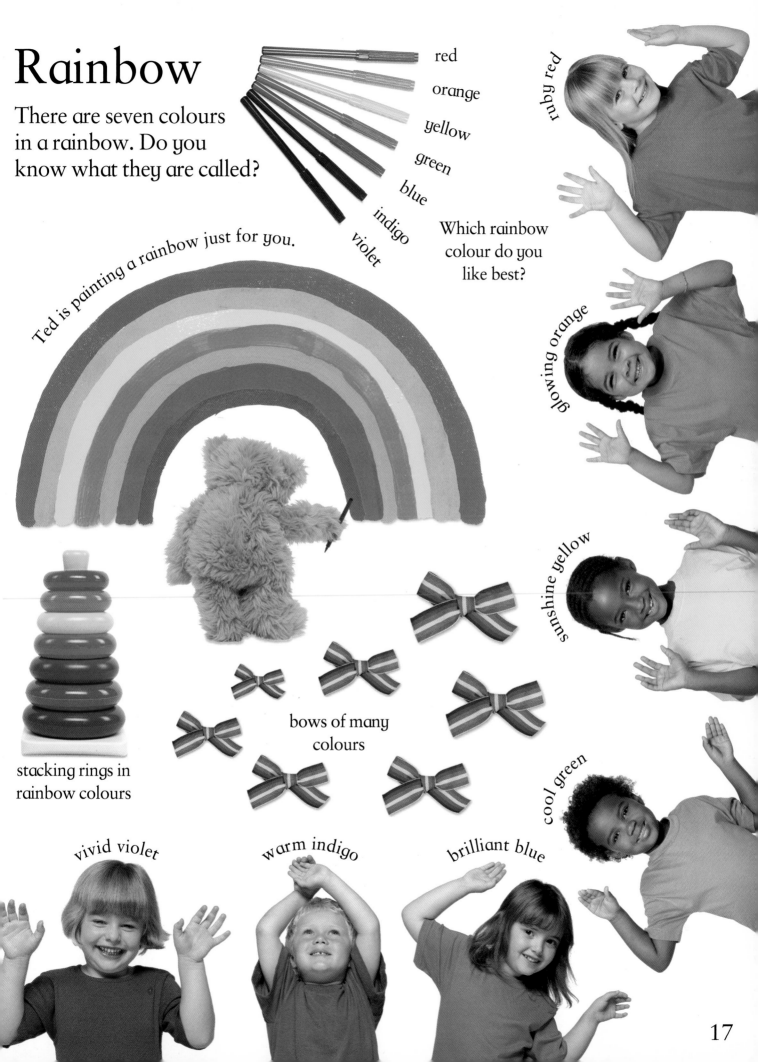

17

Dark to light

Colours can be different shades.
Some are light shades and some
are dark. Can you see the
colours getting lighter?

dark blue

Dangling blue ribbons ...

dark red

Ted's red paper hat ...

dark green

A smart green bow tie ...

dark yellow

Pretty yellow petals ...

light blue

... get lighter and lighter and even lighter.

light red

... gets lighter and lighter and even lighter.

light green

... gets lighter and lighter and even lighter.

light yellow

... get lighter and lighter and even lighter.

19

Light to dark

These pictures show some colours getting darker and darker. Run a finger along the lines of colours from light to dark.

light pink

The pink butterflies ...

light brown

The slithery brown snail's shell ...

light purple

The alien's long hair ...

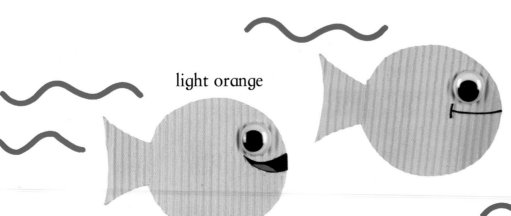

light orange

The splishy, splashy fish ...

dark pink

... get darker and darker and darker.

dark brown

... gets darker and darker and even darker.

dark purple

... gets darker and darker and even darker.

dark orange

... get darker and darker and even darker.

21

Mixing colours

When you mix colours, you make new colours. If you have red, blue and yellow paints, you can make all the colours of the rainbow!

red

blue   yellow

Blue monster is ready to get mixing!

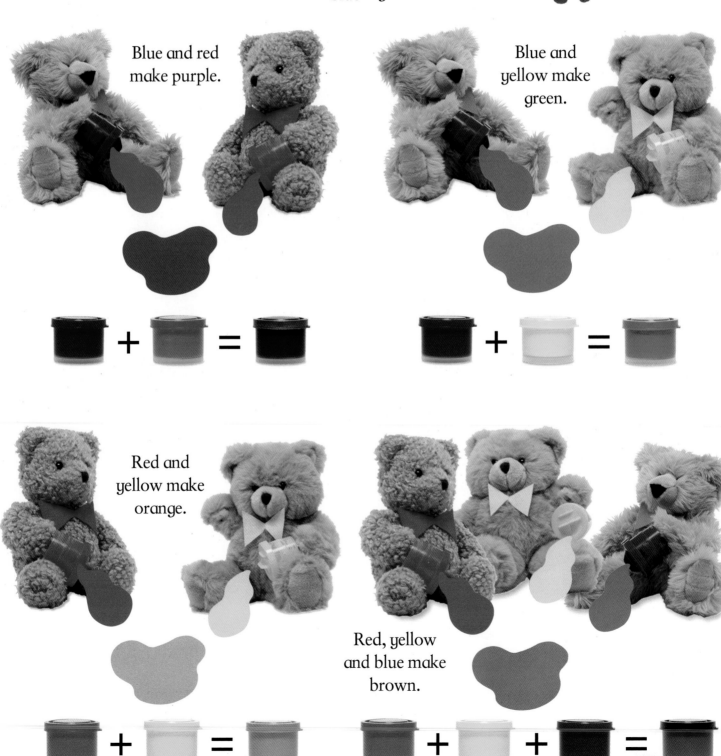

Blue and red make purple.

Blue and yellow make green.

Red and yellow make orange.

Red, yellow and blue make brown.

How do
you make ...

... orange?

... purple?

... green?

... brown?

Try this!

Mixing colours

1. You will need
red, blue and
yellow paints, a
paintbrush and a
container of water.

2. Mix the colours
to make brown,
green, orange
and purple.

3. Use the colours to paint

a brown
teddy

a bright
green pear

an orange stripy cat

a bunch of
purple grapes

Making light colours

Make a paint colour lighter by mixing white into it. A light colour is sometimes called a pale colour.

Blue monster loves mixing light colours.

+ = Red and white make pink.

+ = Green and white make light green.

+ = Brown and white make light brown.

+ = Purple and white make light purple.

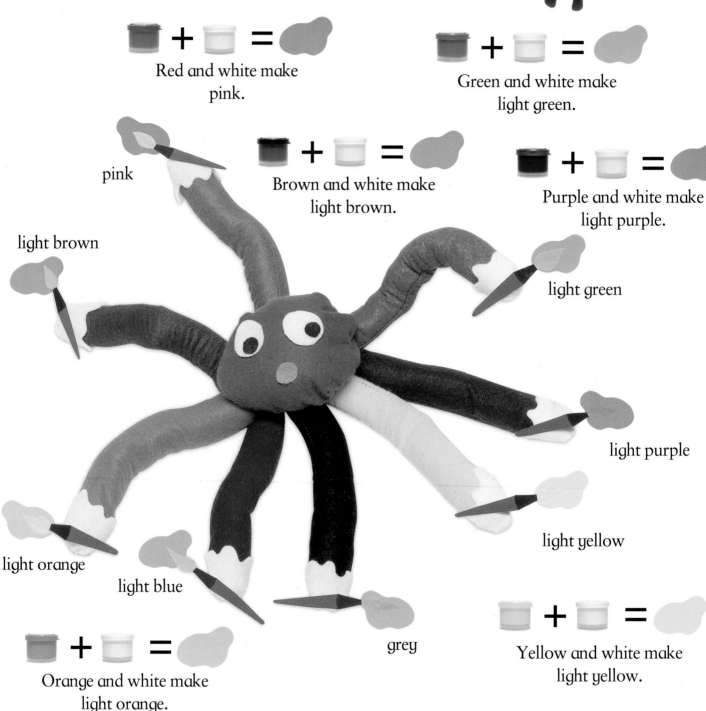

pink

light brown

light green

light purple

light yellow

light orange

light blue

grey

+ = Orange and white make light orange.

+ = Yellow and white make light yellow.

+ = Blue and white make light blue.

+ = Black and white make grey.

24

Try this!

Making light colours

1. You will need red, yellow, blue and white paint, a paintbrush and a container of water.

2. Choose a colour paint and mix it with white.

3. Make light colours to paint

a grey elephant

a pale blue bird

a pink fluffy bunny

a light green bug

Which light and dark colours can you find at home?

dark pink and light pink shoes

red legs

dark purple

light purple

A light blue t-shirt ...

... and a dark blue t-shirt.

dark red legs

25

Colours in nature

The natural world is full of wonderful colours. Sometimes things in nature change colour.

Leaves are green in summer, but ...

... gold and brown in autumn.

Grapes can be green or purple.

Young fir cones are green.

Apples can be different colours.

green apple

red and green apple

Older cones are brown.

red apple

Bees collect nectar from colourful flowers.

Sunlight reflects off the golden beetle and dazzles its enemies.

Flamingos are pink when they eat pink shrimps.

Male ducks are colourful. Can you point to the male duck?

The marbled gecko changes the colour of its skin to match its hiding place.

The three-toed sloth is green because a tiny plant grows in its fur. It does not hurt the sloth.

The chameleon is camouflaged to match the branch.

27

Favourite colours

The children have chosen their favourite colours. Which colour do you like most of all?

Astronaut Ted likes silver because it's shiny.

I like all the colours of the rainbow.

Purple is perfect for my puppet.

Yellow makes me happy.

My monster and I like blue.

I like red. Strawberries are red.

Chocolate-brown is my favourite colour.

My cuddly frog is green.

White is right for me.

I like orange most of all!

My best dance outfit is black.

Glistening gold is my favourite.

Bronze is my favourite colour. My crown is bronze.

Can you guess what colour I like?

29

Treasure hunt

Choose red, green, blue or yellow. Then find, make or draw all the things pictured along the matching coloured line. You can play this alone or with friends.

START HERE

Find, make or draw these red things.

beads

t-shirt

cherry-red cherries

Find, make or draw these green things.

cuddly toy

beetle picture

prickly cactus

Find, make or draw these blue things.

felt-tipped pens

cuddly toy

seaside picture

Find, make or draw these yellow things.

pretty flowers

number two

hat

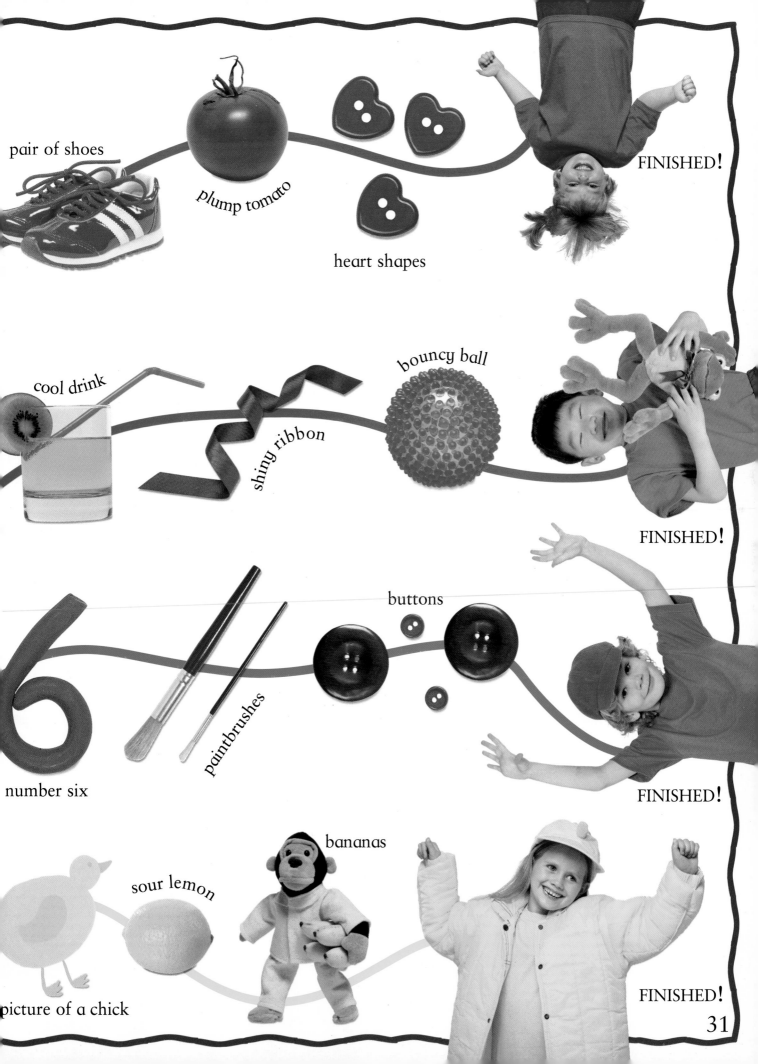

pair of shoes

plump tomato

heart shapes

FINISHED!

cool drink

shiny ribbon

bouncy ball

FINISHED!

buttons

number six

paintbrushes

FINISHED!

bananas

sour lemon

picture of a chick

FINISHED!

This edition is published by Armadillo,
an imprint of Anness Publishing Ltd,
108 Great Russell Street,
London WC1B 3NA;
info@anness.com

www.annesspublishing.com; twitter: @Anness_Books

Anness Publishing has a new picture agency outlet
for images for publishing, promotions or advertising.
Please visit our website www.practicalpictures.com
for more information.

© Anness Publishing Ltd 2015

Publisher: Joanna Lorenz
Senior Editor: Felicity Forster
Educational Consultant: Dr Naima Browne,
    Department of Education, University of London
Photography: John Freeman
Head Stylist: Melanie Williams
Stylist: Ken Campbell
Design: Mike Leaman Design Partners
Production Controller: Ben Worley

PUBLISHER'S NOTE
Although the advice and information in this book are
believed to be accurate and true at the time of going to
press, neither the authors nor the publisher can accept any
legal responsibility or liability for any errors or omissions
that may have been made nor for any inaccuracies nor for
any loss, harm or injury that comes about from following
instructions or advice in this book.

Manufacturer: Anness Publishing Ltd,
108 Great Russell Street, London WC1B 3NA, England
For Product Tracking go to: www.annesspublishing.com/tracking
Batch: 7552-23786-1127

ACKNOWLEDGEMENTS
The publisher would like to thank the following children for
appearing in this book: Africa, Alfie, Ambika, Andrew, April,
Callum, Carolina, Daisy, Faye, Georgina, Lucie, Madison, Philip,
Rebekah, Rosanna, Rubin, Safari, Saffron, Tom.

PICTURE CREDITS
b=bottom, t=top, c=centre, l=left, r=right
© Bruce Coleman Limited: 27tl, 27c, 27bl. © Natural Science
Photos: 27tr, 27tc. © Planet Earth Pictures: 27br.